Contents

Some words are printed in bold, **like this**. You can find out what they mean on page 30. You can also look in the box at the bottom of the page where they first appear.

The last sunset?

The Sun is a star. It is just one star among billions. New stars form and old stars die all the time. What would happen if one day the Sun never rose again? Who would notice if one medium-sized star stopped shining?

You would notice of course. You would notice the darkness right away. You would soon notice the cold! Only a few living things would survive. These living things do not need the Sun's heat and light. But they would only survive for a while.

Is it possible?

There is no danger that the Sun will actually stop shining. It has enough fuel to keep going for billions of years.

The Day the Sun Went Out

Angela Royston

www.raintreepublishers.co.uk
Visit our website to find out more information about **Raintree** books.

To order:
☎ Phone 44 (0) 1865 888112
Send a fax to 44 (0) 1865 314091
Visit the Raintree bookshop at **www.raintreepublishers.co.uk** to browse our catalogue and order online.

First published in Great Britain by Raintree, Halley Court, Jordan Hill, Oxford OX2 8EJ, part of Harcourt Education.
Raintree is a registered trademark of Harcourt Education Ltd.

Editorial: Lucy Thunder, Charlotte Guillian and Harriet Milles
Design: Victoria Bevan and Bigtop
Illustrations: Darren Lingard
Picture Research: Melissa Allison and Debra Weatherley
Production: Camilla Crask

Originated by Dot Gradations Ltd.
Printed and bound in Italy by Printer Trento srl

The paper used to print this book comes from sustainable resources.

ISBN 1 844 43848 1 (hardback)
10 09 08 07 06
10 9 8 7 6 5 4 3 2 1

ISBN 1 844 43941 0 (paperback)
11 10 09 08 07
10 9 8 7 6 5 4 3 2 1

British Library Cataloguing in Publication Data
Royston, Angela
The Day The Sun Went Out: The Sun's Energy
333.7'923
A full catalogue record for this book is available from the British Library.

Acknowledgements
The publishers would like to thank the following for permission to reproduce photographs: Alamy/Nature Picture Library pp. 24–25; Alamy/Steve Bloom Images pp. 12–13; FLPA/Minden Pictures pp. 22–23 (Norbert Wu), 26–27 (Franz Lanting); Getty Images/National Geographic pp. 10–11; Getty Images/Stone pp. 8–9; Holt Studios pp. 14–15; naturepl.com pp. 4–5 (Constantinos Petrinos); NHPA pp. 16–17 (Martin Harvey), 18–19 (Guy Edwardes); NHPA/Image Quest 3-d pp. 20–21.

Cover photograph of a solar eclipse, reproduced with permission of Science Photo Library/David Nunek.

The publishers would like to thank Nancy Harris and Harold Pratt for their assistance in the preparation of this book.

▼*The Sun provides heat and light for life on Earth.*

What makes the Sun shine?

The Sun is about a million times bigger than the Earth. It is an enormous ball of very hot gases. Gas is neither solid nor liquid.

The Sun is made mostly of **hydrogen** gas. Hydrogen burns very easily. The centre (or core) of the Sun is very hot. It is so hot that the hydrogen changes into another gas called **helium**.

When this change happens, a huge amount of **energy** is released. Energy is needed to make things happen. Light and heat energy pours out from the Sun. This energy keeps us alive. If the Sun went out, we would lose all this energy.

Energy

Energy makes things happen. Everything needs energy to move, breathe, or grow.

▼ *The Sun consists mostly of the gas hydrogen.*

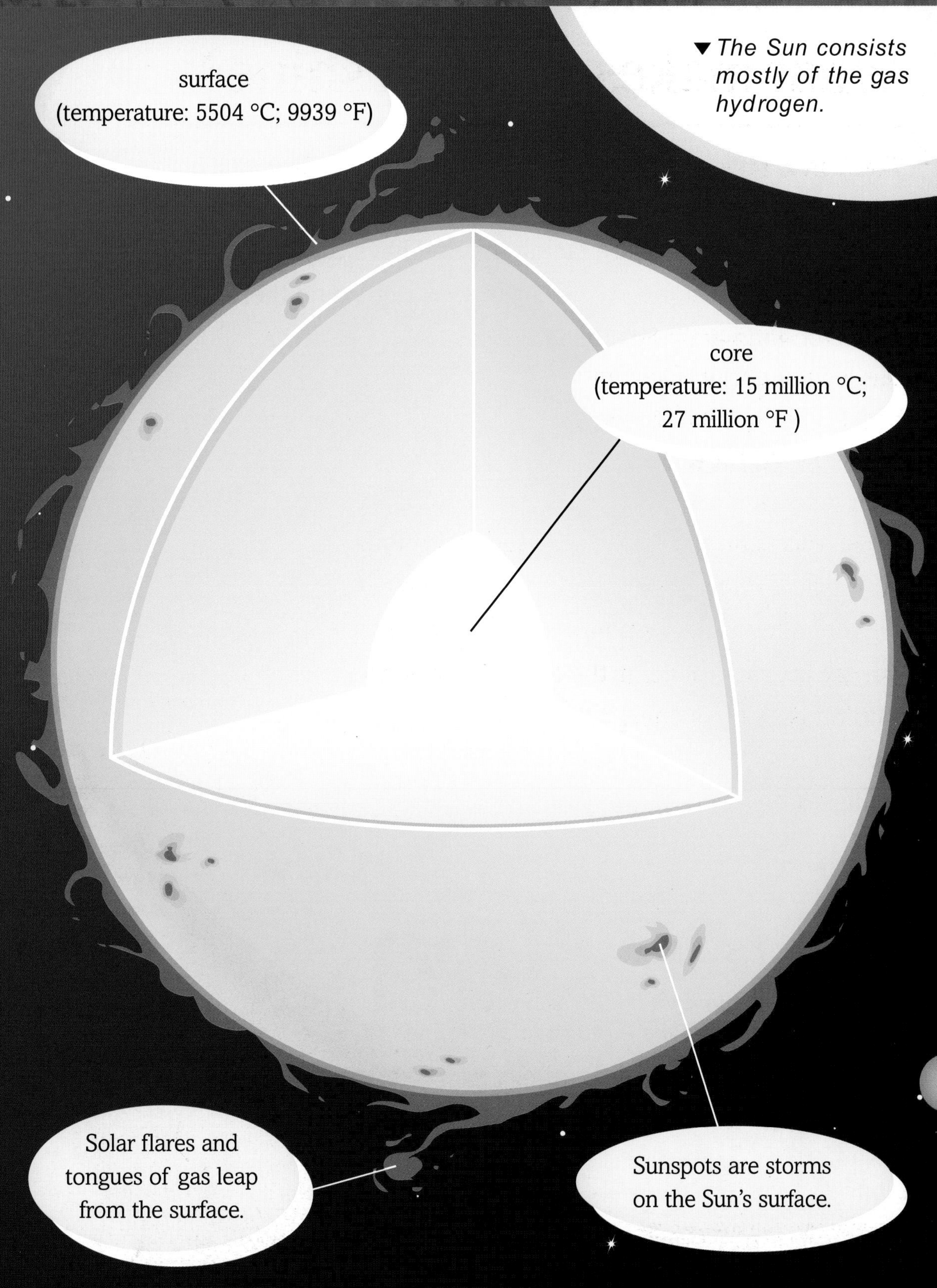

surface
(temperature: 5504 °C; 9939 °F)

core
(temperature: 15 million °C;
27 million °F)

Solar flares and
tongues of gas leap
from the surface.

Sunspots are storms
on the Sun's surface.

Endless night

The Earth spins on its **axis** once every 24 hours. The axis is an imaginary line through the centre of the Earth. The parts of the Earth that are facing the Sun have daylight. The rest of the Earth is in darkness. It is night time there. Places on the Earth move from daylight into darkness, and back into daylight.

Without the Sun, it would always be night time. Imagine what endless night would be like. It would be dark all day at school. You would need electric lights, lamps, or candles to see. Streetlights would be on all the time.

Only the stars would still shine. They would give a small amount of light. But you would not see the Moon. The Moon does not make its own light. Instead it is lit by the light from the Sun.

Sun fact

Sunlight is so strong that it can pass through thick clouds. Otherwise it would be as dark as night on cloudy days.

axis straight line around which something turns

▼At any time, half of the Earth is lit by sunlight and the other half is in darkness.

Big freeze

If the Sun went out, the Earth would cool down. This is because the Sun gives us heat **energy** as well as light. The air, the sea, and the land warm up during the day. At night, one side of the Earth turns away from the Sun's heat. Everything cools down. But the next day, heat from the Sun warms the surface again.

If the Sun stopped shining, the Earth would become colder and colder. Even hot countries would become freezing cold.

Imagine what that would be like. Much of the land would soon be frozen. Rivers and lakes would become solid ice. Ice might even cover your home. It would be hard to walk or drive anywhere.

▼*If the Sun went out, it would always be night time. It would be freezing cold outside – and inside!*

No more rain or snow

If the Sun went out, there would soon be no more rain or snow. This is because the Sun helps to make rain. The Sun heats lakes, rivers, and the sea. Some of the water becomes warm enough to turn to gas. It **evaporates** into the air. This means the water changes into a gas.

Sometimes this gas (**water vapour**) reaches colder air. The gas then changes back to water. It **condenses** to form clouds of tiny water droplets. The droplets join together and become bigger. When they are too big to float in the cloud, they fall as rain.

If there was no sunshine, it would soon be too cold for water to evaporate. There would be no clouds. There would be no more rain or snow.

Sun fact

One reason weather usually changes all the time is because the Earth spins around. Different parts of the Earth get different amounts of sunshine.

condense change from a gas into a liquid
evaporate change from a liquid into a gas
water vapour water in the form of a gas

The water cycle

▲*Water moves around from the air to the surface of the Earth and back again.*

Plants and animals

Green plants use the **energy** of sunlight to make their own food. They make this food in their leaves. This process is called **photosynthesis**.

Photosynthesis happens when the green leaves take in **carbon dioxide** gas from the air. This gas combines with water from the soil. This makes a sugary juice. The juice feeds the whole plant.

Plants cannot make food and grow without light. If you put a plant in a dark cupboard, it will die in a few days.

carbon dioxide gas that is present in the air
photosynthesis the way plants make food using energy from sunlight

Imagine what would happen to plants if the Sun went out. Plants and trees would soon die. Crops such as wheat and rice would die too.

▼*Plants use the energy of sunlight to make sugar in their leaves.*

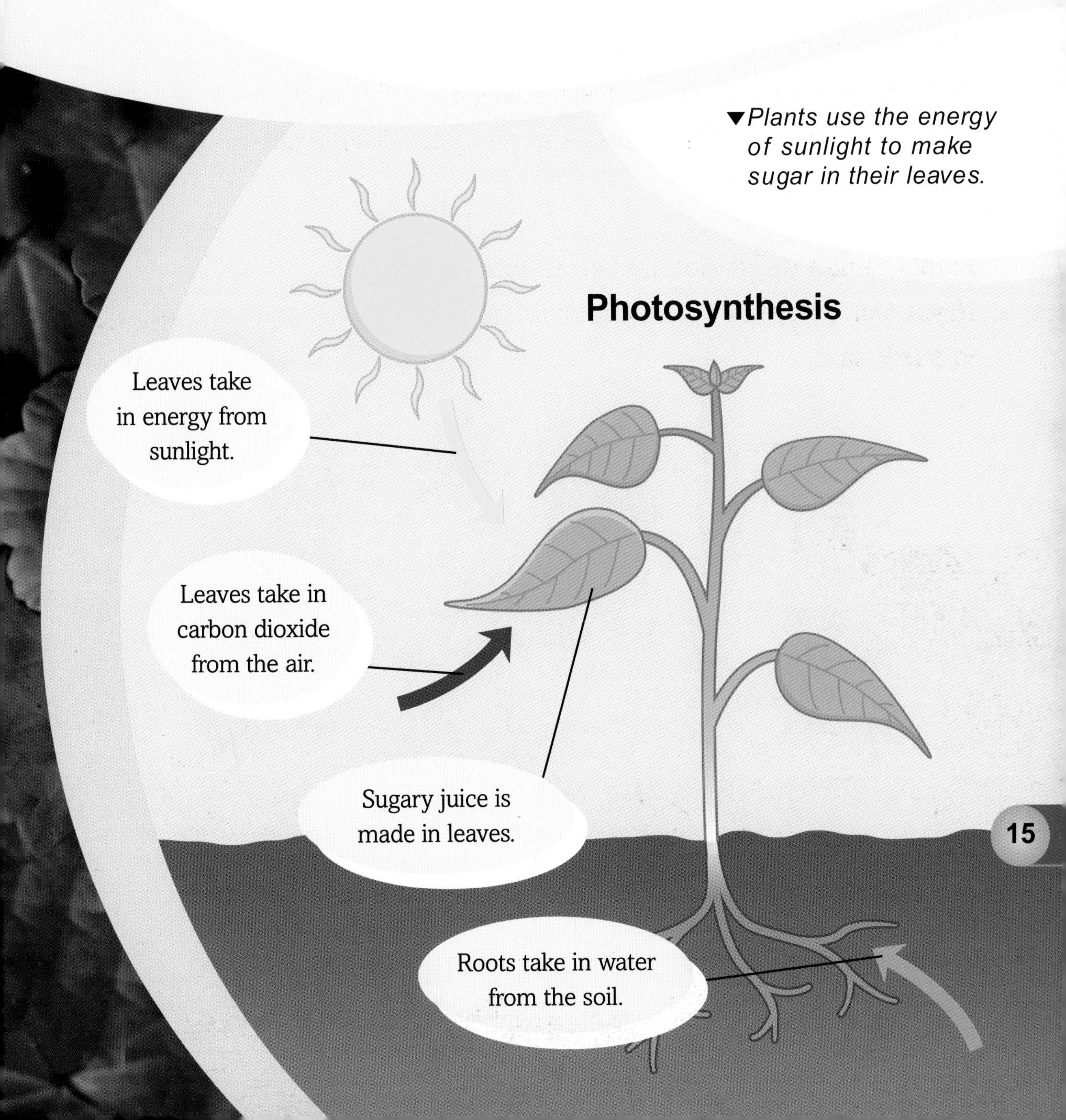

Food links

If the Sun went out and the plants died, animals would die too. Animals are linked to plants and the Sun. They are linked by the food they eat. They are part of a **food chain**. Animals depend on plants for food.

Many animals, such as zebras, only eat plants. If the plants died, these plant-eaters would starve. Some animals, such as lions, only eat meat. They need to eat the plant-eating animals. If there were no plant-eaters, the meat-eaters would starve and die.

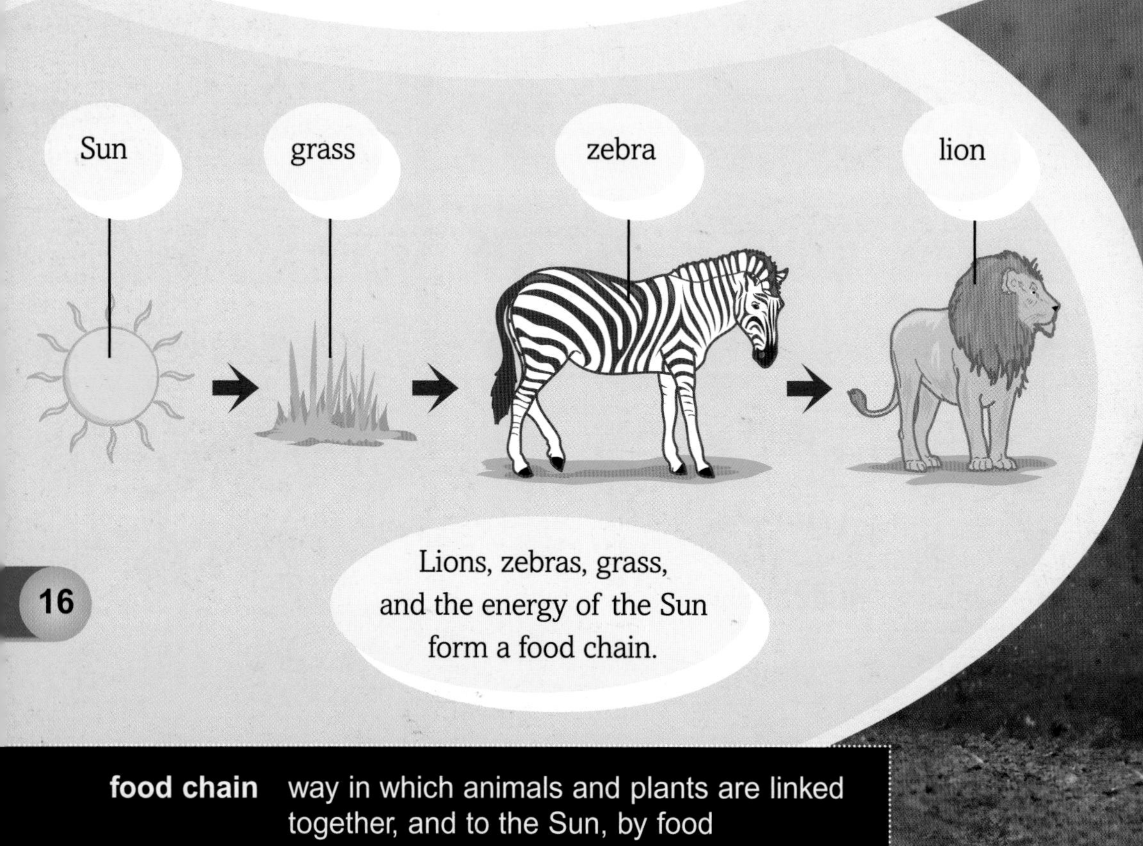

Lions, zebras, grass, and the energy of the Sun form a food chain.

food chain way in which animals and plants are linked together, and to the Sun, by food

scavenger animal that feeds on dead and rotting meat or other waste

Scavengers, such as vultures, eat dead animals. They would feed on the dead meat-eaters. But soon this food would be finished. The scavengers would starve too. Then there would be no living things left.

Living underground

Some animals live underground in the dark. Moles, earthworms, and many insects live in the soil. Some of these animals are almost blind. This is because they never see the light. However, they also need the Sun.

Moles eat earthworms. Earthworms eat fallen leaves. If the Sun stopped shining, leaves would stop growing. There would be no more leaves to fall. Earthworms would have no food. The earthworms would die. Then moles would have nothing to eat.

Moles live ▶ underground. But they still need the Sun to survive.

hibernating falling into a deep sleep to survive cold weather

Frogs, red squirrels, and many other animals survive the cold of winter by **hibernating**. In the summer, they eat lots of food and grow fat. Then they spend the winter months in a deep sleep. Their bodies cool down. They use up very little **energy**. If the Sun went out, it would be much too cold for any of these animals to survive.

In the oceans

The creatures that live in the sea also need the Sun. Most fish and sea animals live in the top of the ocean. Sunlight reaches the top part of the ocean. The Sun warms the water. Deeper down, the water gets colder and colder.

Plants and animals in the ocean are linked together by the food they eat. **Food chains** in the oceans start with tiny plants and animals. These are called **plankton**. They are so small they can only be seen with a **microscope**. Plankton float near the surface of the oceans.

The tiny sea plants use the **energy** of sunlight to make food. They are eaten by small sea animals, such as shrimp. These small animals are eaten by larger fish, like tuna. Larger fish are eaten by large sea animals, such as whales. Without plankton, there would be no food for sea life.

These tiny plankton ▶ have been photographed using a microscope.

microscope machine that makes things look bigger than they really are

plankton tiny plants and animals that float near the surface of the sea

▲ *An ocean food chain.*

Ocean depths

Some types of sea animals live deep in the ocean. The Sun's light does not reach them. But these animals still need the Sun. Some eat dead fish that float down from the sunlit sea above. Others feed on other deep-sea fish.

*These deep-sea viper fish make their own light. But they are part of a **food chain** that relies on the Sun.*

Imagine what would happen if the Sun stopped shining. **Plankton** would die first. Then other sea animals in the top of the ocean would start to die too. Animals at the bottom of the oceans would have plenty to eat. But when there was no life left in the sea above, the deep-sea fish would also die.

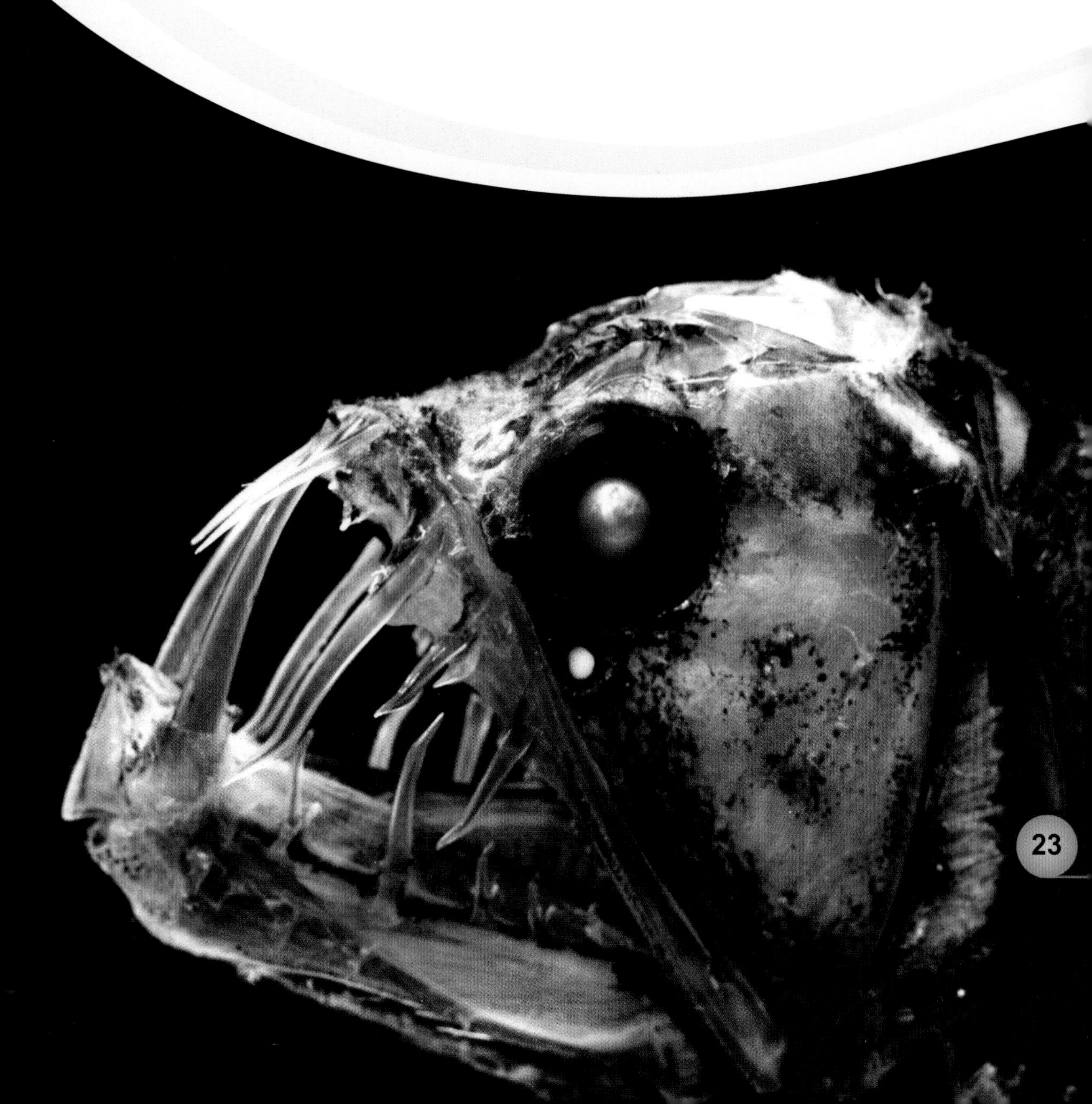

Surviving without sunshine

Some living things can survive without the light or the heat of the Sun. They live at the bottom of the oceans in **thermal vents**.

Thermal vents are cracks in the ocean floor. Sea water trickles down these cracks. The water is heated by hot rocks, deep inside the Earth. Then hot water and gases gush back up through the cracks into the ocean.

Millions of **bacteria** live in the hot water of thermal vents. They feed on chemicals that escape through the cracks. Tube worms, clams, and limpets feed on the bacteria. If the Sun stopped shining, these hot vents would still be there. The strange animals that live in them would survive for a very long time.

These strange animals are called tube worms. They live in thermal vents at the bottom of the ocean. ▶

bacteria tiny forms of life
thermal vent crack in the ocean floor where hot water gushes out

No need to worry!

Don't worry! The Sun will not suddenly stop shining. The Earth will not suddenly be without heat or light. The Sun has been burning for 4500 million years. It has enough fuel left to keep burning for another 5000 million years.

But it is helpful for us to think about what would happen to the Earth if the Sun went out. It shows us how much we need the Sun for light, warmth, and food.

The Sun's energy

*The Sun is mainly made up of a gas called **hydrogen**. The Sun makes **energy** by burning the hydrogen. The Sun is about a million times bigger than the Earth. It can produce a huge amount of energy because it is so enormous and so hot. The temperature in the centre of the Sun (where the energy is made) is 15 million °C (27 million °F).*

Life cycle of a star

The Sun is a star. This diagram shows the life cycle of a star like the Sun.

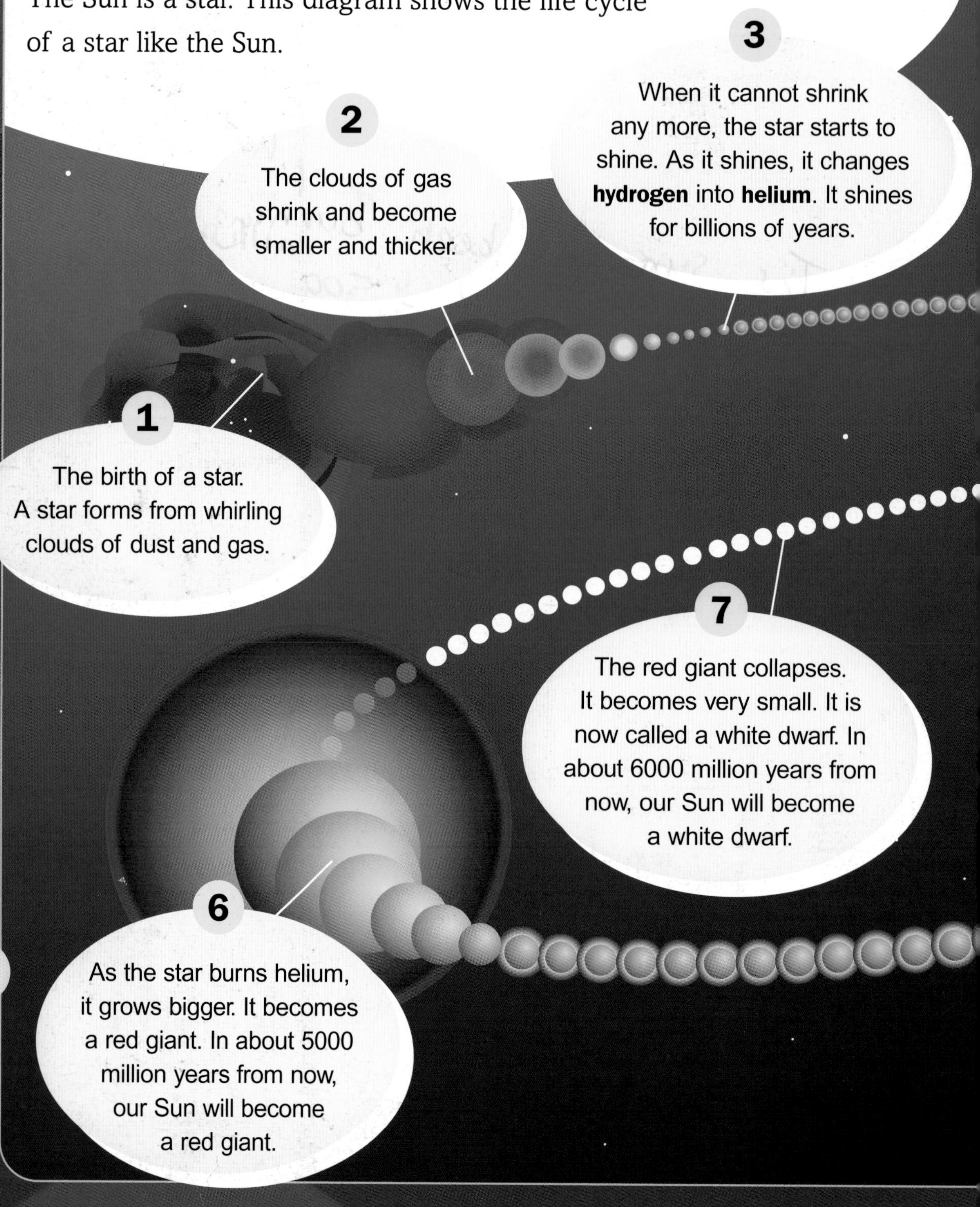

1

The birth of a star. A star forms from whirling clouds of dust and gas.

2

The clouds of gas shrink and become smaller and thicker.

3

When it cannot shrink any more, the star starts to shine. As it shines, it changes **hydrogen** into **helium**. It shines for billions of years.

6

As the star burns helium, it grows bigger. It becomes a red giant. In about 5000 million years from now, our Sun will become a red giant.

7

The red giant collapses. It becomes very small. It is now called a white dwarf. In about 6000 million years from now, our Sun will become a white dwarf.

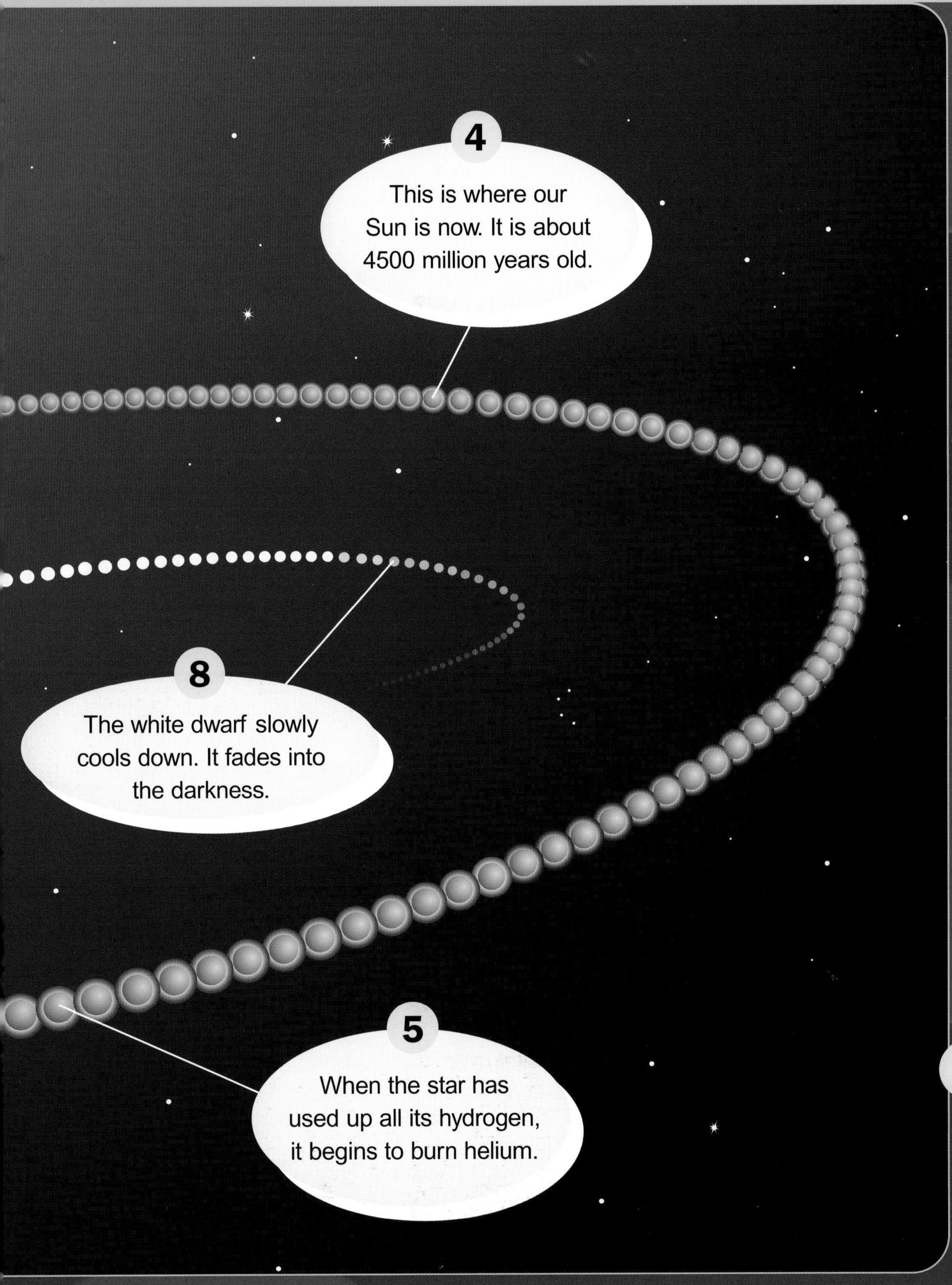

4

This is where our Sun is now. It is about 4500 million years old.

8

The white dwarf slowly cools down. It fades into the darkness.

5

When the star has used up all its hydrogen, it begins to burn helium.

Glossary

axis straight line around which something turns. The Earth's axis is an imaginary line that passes through the centre of the Earth from the North to the South Pole.

bacteria tiny forms of life. A few kinds of bacteria can survive in extreme conditions – in hot springs, under the ice, and in thermal vents.

carbon dioxide gas that is present in the air. Plants take in carbon dioxide to make food. Plants, animals, and humans breathe out carbon dioxide.

condense change from a gas into a liquid. As a gas cools, it condenses more quickly.

energy ability to move something or make something happen. Without energy, nothing could live or grow, and there would be no movement, light, heat, or noise.

evaporate change from a liquid into a gas. The cooler a liquid becomes the slower it evaporates.

food chain way in which animals and plants are linked together, and to the Sun, by food.

helium type of gas. Helium is produced in the core of the Sun.

hibernating falling into a deep sleep to survive cold weather.

hydrogen type of gas. The Sun is mainly made up of hydrogen.

microscope machine that makes things look bigger than they really are.

photosynthesis the way plants make food using energy from sunlight

plankton tiny plants and animals that float near the surface of the sea.

scavenger animal that feeds on dead and rotting meat or other waste. Vultures are a type of scavenger.

thermal vent crack in the ocean floor where hot water gushes out. Bacteria, tube worms, and other animals live in thermal vents. They do not need energy from the Sun.

water vapour water in the form of a gas. Water can exist as a gas, as a liquid, and as solid ice.

Want to know more?

There is a lot more you can find out about the Sun and how we use its energy on Earth:

Books to read

- *Food Chains* series, by Louise and Richard Spilsbury, and Emma Lynch (Heinemann Library, 2004)
  A series of books about food chains in different habitats: deserts, grasslands, mountains, oceans, rainforests, and rivers.
- *The Sun*, by Raman Prinja (Heinemann Library, 2002)
  This book tells you all about the Sun and its life-giving energy.

Websites

- Heinemann Explore: www.heinemannexplore.co.uk.
  Everything you need to know about science and history in KS2.
- Starchild: starchild.gsfc.nasa.gov/docs/StarChild/StarChild.html.
  For more information about the Sun, the planets, and other parts of the Universe.

Why does the weather change at different times of the year? Find out how the Earth moves around the Sun and how it affects the seasons in ***The Day the Earth Stood Still***.

Food chains are everywhere. Find out how food chains in the oceans join up to make food webs in ***Shark Snacks***.

Index